# Language Development Activity Book
## with Standardized Test Practice

1

## ScottForesman

## Accelerating English Language Learning

### Authors

Anna Uhl Chamot

Jim Cummins

Carolyn Kessler

J. Michael O'Malley

Lily Wong Fillmore

### Consultant

George González

ScottForesman

Editorial Offices: Glenview, Illinois
Regional Offices: Sunnyvale, California • Atlanta, Georgia
Glenview, Illinois • Oakland, New Jersey • Dallas, Texas

ISBN 0-673-19693-3

ISBN 0-673-19701-8 [Texas]

4 5 6 7 8 9 10 CR 05 04 03 02 01 00 99 98 97

# Contents

# One or More

Circle the right word for each picture.

dog    dogs

dog    dogs

sister    sisters

sister    sisters

shoe    shoes

shoe    shoes

brother    brothers

brother    brothers

# They or We

Finish the sentence. Write *They* or *We*.

_____

- - - - - - - - - - - - - - - - - - - - - - - -

_____ are having fun.

Add yourself to the picture. Then write *They* or *We*.

_____

- - - - - - - - - - - - - - - - - - - - - - - -

_____ are having fun.

# What's Different?

Look at the two pictures. What is different?
Circle the part of the picture that is different.

# Find and Color

Color the pictures of words whose names begin like *family*.

family

farm

furniture

father

mother

sister

# My Family

Draw pictures of your family.
Show your family members.
Then show what you like to do together.

This is my family.

My family likes to _____.

# Make picture cards.

Cut out the pictures. Tell a friend about who is in the picture and what they are doing.

| eat | listen |
|-----|--------|
| hug | play |
| share | dance |
| write | sing |

# What color is it?

Read the color word.
Color the crayon.

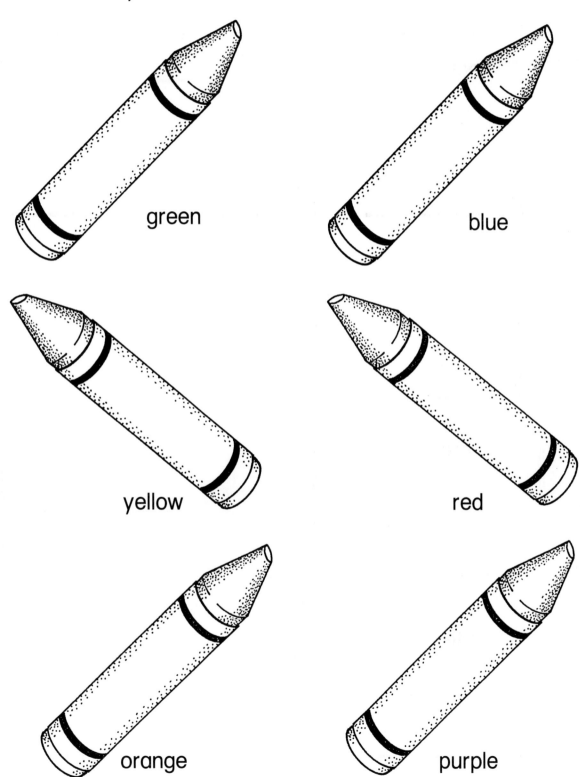

green

blue

yellow

red

orange

purple

## Math Objective: The student will demonstrate an understanding of number concepts.

Sample: 0 1 2 3 4 5 6 7 8 9 10

Each number has a special place. If 3 gets out of line, it always goes back to the same place in the line.

*Before* and *after* are two special words to know.

*Before* means "in front of." The number 1 comes before 2.

*After* means "behind." The number 3 comes after 2.

before                                    after

## Try It

Read the question. Fill in the circle beside the best answer. Choose only one.

1. What number is missing in this line?

   2, 3, ___, 5
   ○ 6
   ○ 1
   ○ 4
   ○ 0

2. What number is missing in this line?

   3, 4, 5, ___
   ○ 3
   ○ 1
   ○ 8
   ○ 6

3. What number comes after 4?
   ○ 5
   ○ 3
   ○ 7
   ○ 1

4. What number comes before 2?

   1, 2, 3, 4, 5, 6, 7, 8
   ○ 3
   ○ 1
   ○ 5
   ○ 7

# What's missing?

Draw the missing picture.

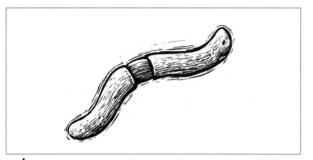

long

longer

tall

taller

big

bigger

small

smaller

Name _____

# Body Parts

Circle the right word for each picture.

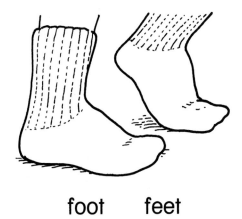

foot     feet

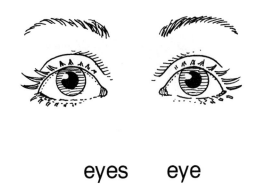

eyes     eye

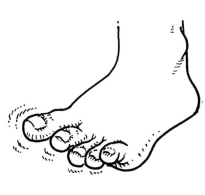

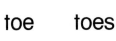

toe     toes

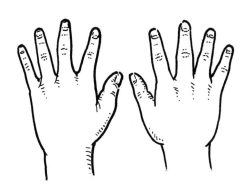

hand     hands

teeth     tooth

ear     ears

© Scott, Foresman and Company

13

Name _____

# In or On?

Look at the picture.
Circle the word that tells about the picture.

in     on          in     on

in     on          in     on

in     on          in     on

14

# Colors

Color each picture. Use the color named.

red

green

yellow

brown

blue

black

Name _____

# Goldy the Dog

Read the sentences.
Circle the words that are names of people and animals.
Then write these words with capital letters.

1. Everybody loves goldy.

_____

------------------------------------

_____

2. daniel loves her.

_____

------------------------------------

_____

3. anna loves her.

_____

------------------------------------

_____

4. mr. johnson loves her.

_____

------------------------------------

_____

5. mrs. garcia loves her.

_____

------------------------------------

_____

6. Even buttons loves her.

_____

------------------------------------

_____

# Same Beginning Sounds

*Goldy giggled at the gorilla.*

Look at the pictures.
Find the pictures that have the same beginning sound as *gorilla*.
Write a *g* under the picture.

_____
- - - - - - - - - - - - - - - - - -
_____

_____
- - - - - - - - - - - - - - - - - -
_____

_____
- - - - - - - - - - - - - - - - - -
_____

_____
- - - - - - - - - - - - - - - - - -
_____

_____
- - - - - - - - - - - - - - - - - -
_____

_____
- - - - - - - - - - - - - - - - - -
_____

Name _____

# Little Gorilla's Friends

These animals loved Little Gorilla.
Write the animal's name below its picture.

| Green Parrot   Red Monkey   Giraffe   Lion   Old Hippo |

_____
- - - - - - - - - - - - - - - - - - - - -
_____

_____
- - - - - - - - - - - - - - - - - - - - -
_____

_____
- - - - - - - - - - - - - - - - - - - - -
_____

_____
- - - - - - - - - - - - - - - - - - - - -
_____

_____
- - - - - - - - - - - - - - - - - - - - -
_____

Who else loved Little Gorilla? _____
Draw its picture.

**18**

# What can they do?

Work with a partner. Match the word with the picture.
Then say what they can do.

write

hit

read

count

make

ride

Name _____

# Reading Objective: The student will determine the meaning of words in a variety of written texts.

Sample:

When you were a baby you were very small. You grew and grew. You got bigger and taller.

Question:

In this story **grew** means

○   change.
○   went to school.
○   got bigger.
○   was grown up.

Name _____

## Try It

Read the passage.
Then answer the questions.

### Little Gorilla

Little Gorilla lived in the forest where he could play in the big tall trees. All of his relatives including his mother, father, grandma, grandpa, aunts, and uncles adored him. Even when he was just one day old they showed how much they adored him by giving him hugs and kisses.

Every year as he grew all of the forest creatures loved him. The Green Parrot and the Red Monkey loved him. Giraffe, Young Elephant, and Old Elephant were all there when he needed them. They all came to his birthday party and sang "Happy Birthday, Little Gorilla!"

1. In this story **forest** means

   ○ green.
   ○ trees.
   ○ animals.
   ○ house.

2. The story uses the word **creatures** to mean

   ○ animals.
   ○ elephants.
   ○ trees.
   ○ parents.

# What did you see?

Draw something you saw in this place.

# To School

Write *I* or *We*.

_____

------------ ride to school.

_____

------------ ride to school.

_____

------------ walk to school.

_____

------------ ride to school.

# School Days

Circle your favorite school day.

Monday     Tuesday     Wednesday     Thursday     Friday

Draw a picture to show what you do on that day.

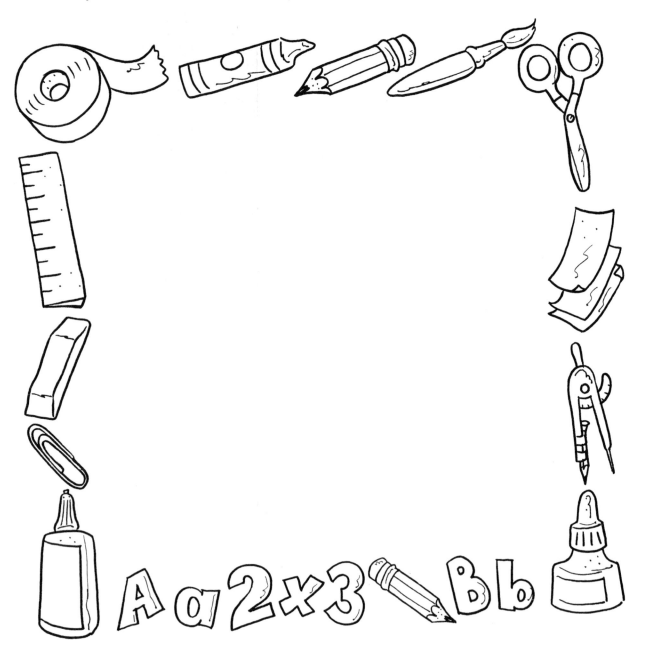

# Where's the class pet?

Find the class pet.

Name the picture.

_____

- - - - - - - - - - - - - - - - - - - - -

_____

Name _____

# How many?

Count how many.
Write the number word.

1 one

2 two

3 three

4 four

_____    _____
- - - - - - - - - - - - - - - - - - - - - - - - - - - - - - - - - - - - - - - - - - - - - - - -
_____    _____

5 five

6 six

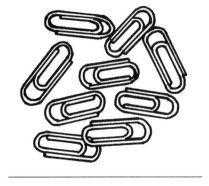
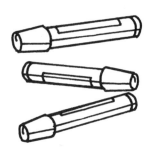

7 seven

_____    _____
- - - - - - - - - - - - - - - - - - - - - - - - - - - - - - - - - - - - - - - - - - - - - - - -
_____    _____

8 eight

9 nine

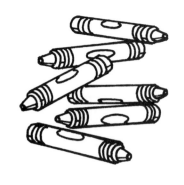

10 ten

_____    _____
- - - - - - - - - - - - - - - - - - - - - - - - - - - - - - - - - - - - - - - - - - - - - - - -
_____    _____

# My Book

Make a book about yourself.
Draw a picture for each sentence.

|  |  |
|---|---|
| This is me. | This is my friend. |
| This is my teacher. | This is how I get to school. |

Name _____

# Questions

Complete each sentence.
Use these question words.

| Who | What | When | Where | Why |
|-----|------|------|-------|-----|

_____ is the boy?

_____ is with the boy?

_____ will the bus come?

_____ is the boy going?

_____ does the boy have a school bag?

Write a question of your own.

_____

_____

28

# School Pictures

Read the words.
Draw a picture.

one school

two teachers

three children

Name _____

# Reading Objective: Arrange events in order.

Sample:

Children get to school in many ways. At our school most students ride the bus. Bus riders need to find a seat quickly when they get on the bus. Many children ride one bus. The bus makes many stops. The last stop in the morning is at the school.

What is the first thing you have to do when you get on the bus?

○ Say hello to the bus driver.
○ Put your backpack down.
○ Wave good-by to your family.
○ Sit down quickly.

The best choice is sit down quickly.

Name _____

# Try It

Read the story. Then answer each question.

My school is fun. I like to go to school every day. The first thing I do is say hello to my teacher. She teaches me lots of things. Every morning we have centers. Some days I do puzzles. The next thing we do is write. I like to write about dinosaurs. After lunch we play outside. In the afternoon we work in our math workbooks. The last thing we do before we go home is read books. This is the best part of the day.

1. Every day after lunch we

○ do alphabet games.
○ write stories.
○ go outside to play.

2. The last thing we do each day at school is

○ read books.
○ get water.
○ play.

3. After centers we always

○ do puzzles.
○ write.
○ read books.

# Block Letters

Name the letters on the blocks.

What letters are missing from the blocks?
Write the letter that belongs on each empty block.

# Learning

Draw a picture of something you learn at school.
Then finish each sentence.

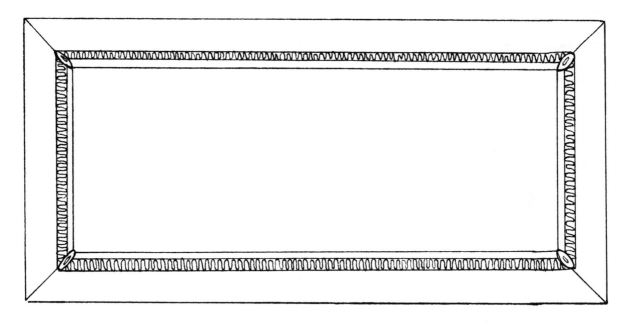

I learn to _____ .

I learn to _____ .

# What are they doing?

speaking

writing

singing

playing

Choose one of the words.
Draw a picture about the word.
Tell about your picture.

# I Can

Put ✓ next to each sentence that tells what you can
do at your school.

_____ I can read.

_____ I can write.

_____ I can play.

_____ I can swim.

_____ I can fish.

_____ I can color.

© Scott, Foresman and Company

Name _____

# Happy or Sad?

happy

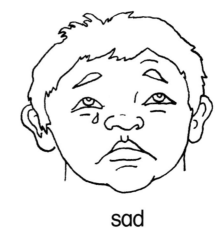

sad

Write a word to finish each sentence.

1. She is _____ .

2. He is _____ .

Draw a happy picture.

# My School

Complete each sentence.
Then draw a picture.

_____
- - - - - - - - - - - - - - - - - - - - - - - - - - - - -

The name of my school is _____.

This is my school.

_____
- - - - - - - - - - - - - - - - - - - - - - - - - - - - -

My teacher's name is _____.

This is my teacher.

Name _____

# Fun at School

| read | write | sing | play | draw | make things |

Choose one thing you like to do at school.
Draw a picture of yourself doing that.
Label your picture.

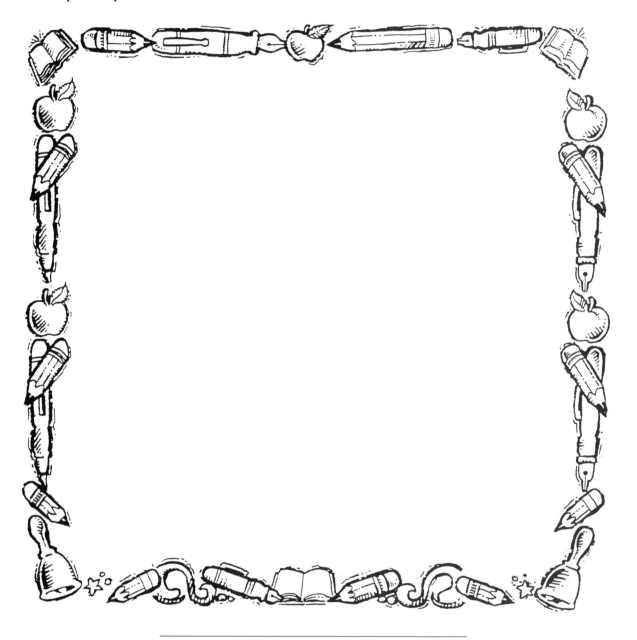

_____

------------------------------------

_____

# At School

Circle the sentence that tells about the picture.

He runs.　　She eats.

He sings.　　She skips.

She walks.　　He listens.

She draws.　　He plays.

Name _____

# Math Objective: Use number line representations for whole numbers.

Sample: Look at the number line.

What number belongs where you see B?

○ 12

○ 10

○ 8

○ 7

If you chose 8, you are right.
The numbers 7 and 8 are both
missing.
The number 8 would go where
you see B.

# Try It

Look at the number line.

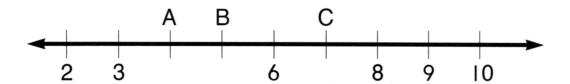

1. What number belongs where you see A?

   ○ 1

   ○ 4

   ○ 5

   ○ 7

2. What number belongs where you see B?

   ○ 5

   ○ 7

   ○ 4

   ○ 1

3. What number belongs where you see C?

   ○ 4

   ○ 1

   ○ 7

   ○ 5

Name _____

# Who and Where

Read the story. Then answer the questions.

Grant lives in a busy neighborhood. His friend Pedro lives in the house next door. One day Grant went outside. He met his friend Pedro. Then he met Sam. Pedro, Sam, and Grant played together at Grant's house.

1. Who is the story about?

_____

- - - - - - - - - - - - - - - - - - - - - - - - - - - - - - -

_____

2. Where does Grant live?

_____

- - - - - - - - - - - - - - - - - - - - - - - - - - - - - - -

_____

3. Who lives in the house next door?

_____

- - - - - - - - - - - - - - - - - - - - - - - - - - - - - - -

_____

4. Who did Grant meet?

_____

- - - - - - - - - - - - - - - - - - - - - - - - - - - - - - -

_____

5. Where did they play?

_____

- - - - - - - - - - - - - - - - - - - - - - - - - - - - - - -

_____

Name _____

# Annie's Neighborhood

Annie is on her way to school.

Color the 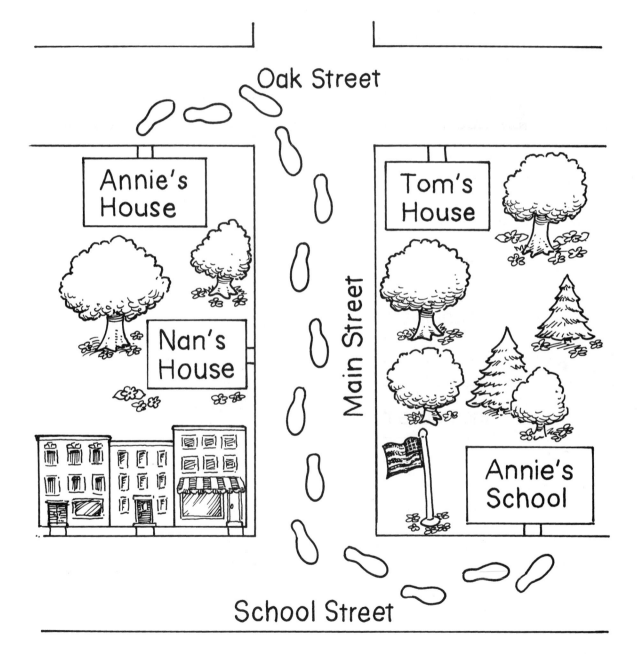 to show how she goes to school.

Name _____

# Special Names

Special names begin with capital letters.
Write a special street name to finish each sentence.

Ben lives on
_____
_____ .

Sara lives on
_____
_____ .

Billy lives on
_____
_____ .

Mary lives on
_____
_____ .

# Opposites

Write words that go with each picture.

| stop | left | go straight |
|------|------|-------------|
| go | right | turn |

_____  _____

- - - - - - - - - - - - - - - - -  - - - - - - - - - - - - - - - - -

_____  _____

- - - - - - - - - - - - - - - - -  - - - - - - - - - - - - - - - - -

_____  _____

- - - - - - - - - - - - - - - - -  - - - - - - - - - - - - - - - - -

# Begin with a capital!

Write each sentence. Begin it with a capital letter.

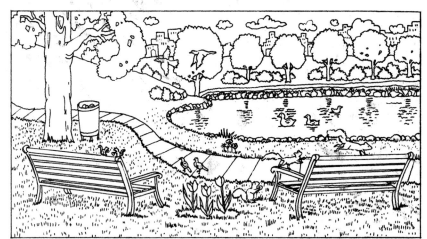

1. squirrels look for nuts.

_____

-------------------------------------------------

_____

2. how many chipmunks are there?

_____

-------------------------------------------------

_____

3. two birds fly in the park.

_____

-------------------------------------------------

_____

4. are there any ducks in the pond?

_____

-------------------------------------------------

_____

5. two pigeons are in the park.

_____

-------------------------------------------------

_____

Write a sentence about the ducks.
Begin your sentence with a capital letter.

-------------------------------------------------

_____

Name _____

# Animal Labels

Write a label for each picture.

| kitten | puppy | hamster | cat | rabbit | bird |
|--------|-------|---------|-----|--------|------|
| kittens | puppies | hamsters | cats | rabbits | birds |

_____

_ _ _ _ _ _ _ _ _ _ _ _

_____

_ _ _ _ _ _ _ _ _ _ _ _

_____

_ _ _ _ _ _ _ _ _ _ _ _

_____

_ _ _ _ _ _ _ _ _ _ _ _

_____

_ _ _ _ _ _ _ _ _ _ _ _

_____

_ _ _ _ _ _ _ _ _ _ _ _

Name _____

# Tell what you see in the picture.

Look at the picture.
Then complete the sentence.
Use these words.

| above | near | in | on |
|-------|------|-----|-----|

1.
The cat is _____ the chair.

2.
The dog is _____ the door.

3.
The clock is _____ the
flowers.

4.
The puppy was _____ the
basket.

# Find Your Way to School

Mark a way to get to school. Then work with a partner.
Give your partner directions. Use these words.

| go | stop | street | turn | straight |
|----|------|--------|------|----------|
| house | right | left | school | |

# Math Objective: Demonstrate an understanding of geometric properties. Evaluate to determine if solution is reasonable.

Read the problem.
Then estimate an answer that makes sense.

Sample:

Adrienne is having a cookout. Her friends will probably eat 2 hot dogs each. There are 8 hot dogs in a package. How many packages should her mother buy for Adriene and her 2 friends to eat?

○ 3

○ I

○ 8

○ 2

If you guessed I package, you're right. That is the best answer. If Adrienne and her friends each eat 2 hot dogs, I package will be enough.

## Try It

Read the problem. Then answer the question.

1. How many sides does this shape have?

○ 4

○ 6

○ 5

○ 2

2. Which figure is a square?

○

○

○

○

3. Anna has 2 friends. Her friends like to eat cookies. Anna and her friends can eat 6 cookies each. Anna has invited her friends for cookies and juice. Each package holds 6 cookies. How many packages should Anna buy?

○ 3

○ 1

○ 8

○ 2

# Words That Tell Where

Circle the words that tell where the animal lives.

Where does the rabbit live?

in a tree

in a field

Where does the toad live?

in a tree

in a pond

Where does the bird live?

in a tree

in a pond

Where does the turtle live?

in a tree

in a pond

# Action Words

The action word tells what the animals do.
Draw a line under the action word in each sentence.

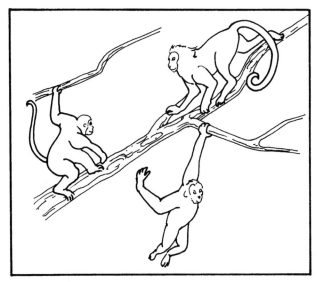

Monkeys swing in the trees.

Rabbits hop in the woods.

Lions roar in the jungle.

Seals swim in the pool.

# Action Words with -s

Action words that tell what one animal does end with -s.
Draw a line under the action word in each sentence.
Then write the action word.

1. The bird builds a nest in a tree.

2. One monkey climbs in trees.

3. A seal swims in water.

4. This lion rests in tall grass.

# Animal Baby Match-Up

Match each animal with its baby.

**bear**

**calf**

**cat**

**puppy**

**horse**

**fawn**

**dog**

**cub**

**cow**

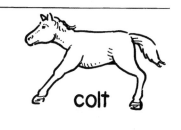

**colt**

**deer**

**kitten**

# Taking Care of Pets

Choose a pet.

| | | | | | |
|---|---|---|---|---|---|
| dog | cat | turtle | fish | bird | hamster |

Draw a picture of this pet.
Label your picture.

Finish each sentence.

| | | | | |
|---|---|---|---|---|
| food | eat | play | run | sleep |
| happy | | for walks | | to the vet |

1. I feed the pet

_____

----------------------------------

_____ .

2. I take the pet

_____

----------------------------------

_____ .

3. I make the pet

_____

----------------------------------

_____ .

# What will happen?

Look at the pictures.
Complete each sentence.
Tell what will happen.

1. Monica _____ _____ walk her dog.

2. Xavier _____ give his cat the toy.

3. Akiko _____ give her dog water.

4. The dog _____ sleep in its bed.

Look at this picture. Write what will happen.

# Animal Labels

Label each picture with its name.

| | |
|---|---|
| bird | giraffe |
| cat | seal |
| dog | squirrel |

_____
- - - - - - - - - - - - - - - -
_____

_____
- - - - - - - - - - - - - - - -
_____

| | |
|---|---|
| camel | opossum |
| caterpillar | toad |
| monkey | turtle |

_____

_____

_____

_____

_____

_____

# Reading Objective: Identify supporting ideas in a variety of written texts.

Read the passage.

Look back in the passage to help you answer the question.

Sample:

All animals have a special place to live.
Turtles live in ponds. Rabbits dig holes in
the ground. Birds live in nests in trees.
Animals that live with people are called pets.
Cats and dogs are pets.
Some people also have other kinds of pets.

Where do birds live?

○ in the forest.

○ in nests in trees.

○ in birdhouses.

○ in zoos.

The passage states *nests in trees.* The passage does not mention the other places.

## Try It

Read the passage.
Then answer the questions.

### A Tree is a Home

Many animals use trees for homes. Caterpillars live on the leaves. Raccoons, squirrels, and owls live in the holes of trees. Squirrels also use the branches of trees. Opossums like to hang upside down on branches.

Birds use trees as a place to build their nests. Some birds build big nests. Other birds build small nests.

1. Where do raccoons live?
○ in the forest.
○ in holes of trees.
○ in birdhouses.
○ in zoos.

2. Opossums use branches to
○ eat leaves.
○ hang upside down.
○ store their food.
○ build nests.

3. Why is a tree a good place for animals to make their homes?
○ It is in the forest.
○ Birds nest there.
○ Trees are big.
○ Trees have many parts.

Name _____

# Feeling Safe

Who helps keep you safe in each place?
Draw a line to match the person to the place.

crossing guard

home

lifeguard

street

mother and father

school

teacher

swimming pool

# Word Makers!

Finish each sentence.
Add *er* to the underlined word to make a new word.

If you <u>sing</u>, you are a

_____

- - - - - - - - - - - - - - - - -

_____ .

If you <u>climb</u>, you are a

_____

- - - - - - - - - - - - - - - - -

_____ .

If you <u>read</u>, you are a

_____

- - - - - - - - - - - - - - - - -

_____ .

If you <u>build</u> things, you are a

_____

- - - - - - - - - - - - - - - - -

_____ .

# Pass!

Look at each picture.
Then check the two sentences that tell about the picture.

_____ The girl waits for the cars to pass.

_____ The girl waits for the cars to go by.

_____ The girl waits for lunch.

_____ I hand the note to my friend.

_____ I write a note to my friend.

_____ I pass the note to my friend.

_____ Please pass the milk.

_____ Please hand me the milk.

_____ Please drop the milk.

_____ The girls pass by the house.

_____ The girls stop to talk.

_____ The girls go by the house.

# Rules! Rules! Rules!

Look at the picture.
Then read both sentences.
Circle the sentence written like a rule.

Do not feed the bears.

Bears eat nuts and berries.

The man walks on the grass.

Keep off the grass.

Always wear your seat belt.

The family rides in the car.

The lady walks the dog.

Never pet a strange dog.

Write a rule to go with this picture.

_____
- - - - - - - - - - - - - - - - - - - - - - - - - - - - - - -
_____

# Finish the Rhyme

Read these lines.
Choose the word that rhymes to finish the second line.
Write the word.

When you are sick in bed,
It's nice to have a pillow
under your

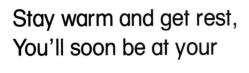

_____

- - - - - - - - - - - - - - - - - - - -

_____ .

head   neck

Stay warm and get rest,
You'll soon be at your

_____

- - - - - - - - - - - - - - - - - - - -

_____ .

school   best

A get-well card or letter
Can make you feel a lot

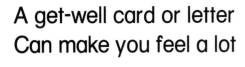

_____

- - - - - - - - - - - - - - - - - - - -

_____ .

better   stronger

# What did they say?

Draw a line to match the sentence with the person who said it.

"Look!" said the doctor.

"Good!" said the nurse.

"Fine!" said the lady with
the alligator purse.

"Yes!" said Tiny Tim.

Name _____

# People, Places, and Safety

Draw a picture to go with the word.

home

mother

school

teacher

Name ______________________________

crossing guard

street

park ranger

park

Write a sentence about who keeps you safe.

Name _____

# Math Objective: Use the operation of subtraction to solve problems.

Sample:

Marisol has 12 fish in her aquarium. She gives 4 fish to her friend Anna. How many fish does she have left?

- ○ 16
- ○ 8
- ○ 6
- ○ 9

Marisol had 12 fish and gave away 4. The number sentence is 12 − 4 = 8. She has 8 fish left.

Name _____

## Try It

Read each question carefully.
Solve the problem. Mark your choice.

1. Jiame liked to play cars.
He had 10 cars. He put 5 cars
on the steps. The other ____
cars were on the grass.

- ○ 14
- ○ 6
- ○ 15
- ○ 5

2. Which number sentence
does the picture show?

- ○ $4 + 2 = 6$
- ○ $4 - 2 = 2$
- ○ $2 - 2 = 0$
- ○ $2 + 2 = 4$

3. Yesenia has 10 flowers.
She gives 5 flowers to Maria.
How many flowers does she
have left?

- ○ 15
- ○ 6
- ○ 4
- ○ 5

4. Which number sentence
does the picture show?

- ○ $5 - 2 = 3$
- ○ $3 - 2 = 1$
- ○ $5 - 3 = 2$
- ○ $3 + 2 = 5$

# Who are they?

Read the first sentence.
Then read the second sentence.
Find the word that takes the place of
the underlined words.
Circle the word.

The cats are sleeping.
They are sleeping.

The girls are playing.
They are playing.

The children are skating.
They are skating.

The boys are swimming.
They are swimming.

The girls are drinking milk.

_____

------------------------------

_____ are drinking milk.

# Opposites

Look at the pictures.
Draw a line between the words that show opposites.

1.

yes

happy

2.

sad

dirty

3.

clean

no

Then write the opposites below.

1. _____

2. _____

3. _____

Name _____

# Food Talk

Read the sentence.
Circle the picture that shows what the sentence is about.

This is corn.

This is a banana.

This is an apple.

This is a carrot.

This is meat.

This is rice.

This is milk.

This is an egg.

Complete the sentence. Tell two things you like to eat.

I like to eat _____ and _____ .

74

# Days of the Week

Name the days of the week.
Write the missing day on the line.

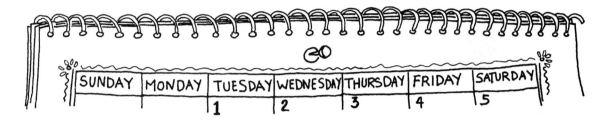

_____
- - - - - - - - - - - - - - - - - - - - - - - - - - - - - - -
1. Monday _____ Wednesday

_____
- - - - - - - - - - - - - - - - - - - - - - - - - - - - - - -
2. Thursday _____ Saturday

_____
- - - - - - - - - - - - - - - - - - - - - - - - - - - - - - -
3. Tuesday _____ Thursday

_____
- - - - - - - - - - - - - - - - - - - - - - - - - - - - - - -
4. Sunday _____ Tuesday

_____
- - - - - - - - - - - - - - - - - - - - - - - - - - - - - - -
5. Friday _____ Sunday

Pick a day of the week.
Write what you like to do on that day.

_____        _____
- - - - - - - - - - - - - - - - - -        - - - - - - - - - - - - - - - - - - - -
On _____ I like to _____.

# End with a Period

Write each sentence.
End each sentence with a period (.).

1. Allie Alligator saw giraffes play basketball

_____
- - - - - - - - - - - - - - - - - - - - - - - - - - - - - - - - - - - - -
_____

_____
- - - - - - - - - - - - - - - - - - - - - - - - - - - - - - - - - - - - -
_____

2. She saw the foxes run

_____
- - - - - - - - - - - - - - - - - - - - - - - - - - - - - - - - - - - - -
_____

_____
- - - - - - - - - - - - - - - - - - - - - - - - - - - - - - - - - - - - -
_____

3. She saw gorillas climb the ropes

_____
- - - - - - - - - - - - - - - - - - - - - - - - - - - - - - - - - - - - -
_____

_____
- - - - - - - - - - - - - - - - - - - - - - - - - - - - - - - - - - - - -
_____

Choose one sentence you wrote.
Draw a picture.
Show what is happening.

# Rhyme Time

Look at the picture.
Then complete the rhyme.

| cool | run | gym | fall |
|------|-----|-----|------|

 Allie had no fun
_____

when she went for a _____.

 She missed the ball
_____

and she did _____.

 She went for a swim
_____

at the _____.

 In the pool
_____

she was so _____.

Name _____

# Feeling Healthy

Put the word where it belongs.

| apples | bike | skate |
|--------|------|-------|
| bananas | corn | play |
| swim | carrots | run |

food                          exercise

_____           _____

_____           _____

_____           _____

_____           _____

_____           _____

_____           _____

_____           _____

_____           _____

_____           _____

_____           _____

_____           _____

_____           _____

Draw a picture of a fruit you like to eat. Label your picture.

_____

_____

# Healthy Match

Find the picture that goes with each word.
Write the word below the picture.

| wash | skate | bike | carrots |
|------|-------|------|---------|
| run  | swim  | bananas | sleep |

_____

- - - - - - - - - - - - -

_____

_____

- - - - - - - - - - - - -

_____

_____

- - - - - - - - - - - - -

_____

_____

- - - - - - - - - - - - -

_____

_____

- - - - - - - - - - - - -

_____

_____

- - - - - - - - - - - - -

_____

_____

- - - - - - - - - - - - -

_____

_____

- - - - - - - - - - - - -

_____

Name _____

# Reading Objective: Analyze information in order to make conclusions.

Sample:

Do you want to feel healthy? There are three things that will help you. Every night you need at least 8 hours of sleep. You need to exercise every day to help your body feel better. You also need to eat food from all the basic food groups each day.

1. What should you eat every day to feel healthy?

○   cake

○   pie

○   fruits and vegetables

○   candy

Fruits and vegetables would be the best answer. The passage says food from all the basic food groups should be eaten each day. We know that fruits and vegetables are the kinds of foods we need most.

Name _____

## Try It

First read each question. Then read the story.
Answer each question.

Allie had heard that the gym was a healthy place to go every day. One day she decided to go to the gym. Allie saw giraffes playing basketball. She saw foxes running laps. She saw gorillas climbing ropes. After watching for a while, Allie decided to do the exercises too. First she tried to climb the rope. Next she tried to play basketball. Then she tried running laps. She could not do any of the exercises. At last Allie saw the pool. She put on her suit. She jumped in the pool. "Swimming is the best exercise for me!" she said.

1. Allie thought the gym was

○ near her house.

○ fun.

○ closed for the day.

○ a good exercise place.

2. How did Allie feel when she swam?

○ sad

○ mad

○ scared

○ happy

# Action Words

Look at the picture.
Then write the word to finish the sentence.

| see | smell | hear | touch | taste |
|-----|-------|------|-------|-------|
| sees | smells | hears | touches | tastes |

1. They _____ the flowers.

2. He _____ the apple.

3. She _____ the music.

4. They _____ her picture.

5. She _____ the soft kitten.

Name _____

# Senses and Body Parts

Label the picture.
Write the word that names each body part.

| eye | hand | ear | leg | nose |
|-----|------|-----|-----|------|

Read the chant.

I see with my eyes.

I hear with my ears.

I taste with my tongue.

I smell with my nose.

I touch with my hands.

Name _____

# Use your senses.

Read the question.
Circle the picture that answers the question.

What is round?

What is loud?

What smells good?

What tastes salty?

What feels smooth?

What feels bumpy?

Name _____

# One or More Than One?

Look at the picture.
Circle the word that matches the picture.

1.  hand          hands

2.  flower          flowers

3.  eye          eyes

4.  kitten          kittens

5.  ear          ears

6.  lemon          lemons

7.  cap          caps

8. 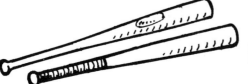 bat          bats

# Loud and Soft

Read these lines to a friend.
Which words do you say loudest?

I MUST get to sleep.
I have to get up EARLY.
WHAT'S keeping me up?

Draw a picture to go with the caption.
Tell about your picture.

I am so VERY tired.

# What's keeping Mr. Bear awake?

Color five things that make noise.

# What happened?

Use the word *went* to complete the story.
Then draw a picture about your story.

_____

A bear _____ to see his friend.

_____

The bear _____ up the mountain.

_____

The bear _____ over the mountain.

_____

The bear _____ to his friend's house.

His friend was not at home.

_____

So the bear _____ up the mountain.

_____

The bear _____ over the mountain.

_____

And the bear _____ home.

Name _____

# Which Sense?

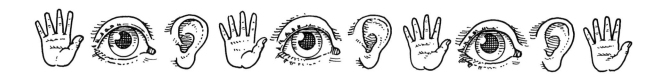

Draw a line to match the sense with the body part.

| | |
|---|---|
| see | ears |
| hear | hands |
| taste | nose |
| smell | eyes |
| touch | tongue |

Finish each sentence.

I use my _____ to smell a flower.

I use my _____ to see my friends.

I use my _____ to taste an apple.

I use my _____ to hear a bird.

I use my _____ to touch a kitten.

Name _____

## Math Objectives: Estimate solutions to a problem. Determine solutions to solve a problem.

Sample: Read the problem.

Andy saw 6 birds in a tree.

He then saw 3 more birds in the tree.

What is a reasonable guess for the total number
of birds in the tree?

○ more than 11

○ between 8 and 10

○ less than 6

○ between 3 and 5

If you chose between 8 and 10 you are right.

6 birds plus 3 birds equals 9 birds in the tree.

The number 9 is between 8 and 10.

## Try It

Read each problem. Answer the question.

1. Marco had 6 marbles. Joseph gave him some more. Now Marco has 10 marbles. Which sentence tells this story?

   ○ ☐ + 6 = 10

   ○ 6 + 10 = ☐

   ○ 10 + 6 = ☐

   ○ 4 + ☐ = 6

2. Alex lives 10 blocks from school. Carlos lives 12 blocks from school. Carlos lives how many more blocks from school than Alex?

   ○ 3                    ○ 1

   ○ 2                    ○ 5

3. Maria saw 5 cars in the school parking lot. She saw 4 more cars drive into the parking lot. What is a reasonable guess for the total number of cars in the parking lot?

   ○ more than 12         ○ less than 3

   ○ between 8 and 10     ○ between 3 and 5

# Very Well

These children do things *very well*.
Read each sentence.
Draw a line to the picture it tells about.

1. Rolando hears very well.

2. Jana sees very well.

3. Nanette runs very well.

4. Paul plays very well.

5. Eddie sings very well.

Tell what you do *very well*. Draw a picture.

_____

_____

- - - - - - - - - - - - - - - - - - - - - - -

I _____ very well.

# Use capital letters.

Write each sentence.
Use a capital letter to begin the sentence.
End the sentence with a period.

1. a bat can hear very well

_____

- - - - - - - - - - - - - - - - - - - - - - - - - - -

_____ .

2. a dolphin can hear too

_____

- - - - - - - - - - - - - - - - - - - - - - - - - - -

_____ .

3. some animals have big ears

_____

- - - - - - - - - - - - - - - - - - - - - - - - - - -

_____ .

Write a sentence.

Tell about the elephant's ears.

_____

- - - - - - - - - - - - - - - - - - - - - - - - - - -

_____ .

Write a sentence about the rabbit.

Tell about the rabbit's ears.

_____

- - - - - - - - - - - - - - - - - - - - - - - - - - -

_____ .

Name _____

# Beanbag Chart

Mark how many times you catch the beanbag.
How many times did you catch the beanbag?

| | number of times beanbag was caught |
|---|---|
| using 1 eye | |
| using 2 eyes | |

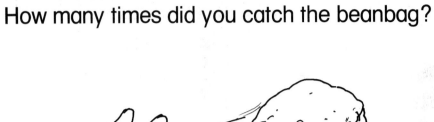

_____

- - - - - - - - - - - - - - - - - - - - - - - -

_____

Name _____

# Numerals and Number Words

| | | | |
|---|---|---|---|
| 1 | one | 6 | six |
| 2 | two | 7 | seven |
| 3 | three | 8 | eight |
| 4 | four | 9 | nine |
| 5 | five | 10 | ten |

Look at the picture.
Draw a line under the number word that tells about it.
Then write the numeral.

_____

two giraffes _____

_____

eight fish _____

_____

three rabbits _____

_____

five frogs _____

_____

four turkeys _____

_____

six cats _____

© Scott, Foresman and Company

Name _____

# Questions and Answers

Look at the underlined words.
Some words in the question are used in the answer.

  Question: How many <u>little</u> <u>cars</u> do you <u>see</u>?
  Answer: I <u>see</u> two <u>little</u> <u>cars</u>.

Write an answer for each question.
Use words from the question in the answer.

1. How many fire engines do you see?

I _____ two

_____

_____ .

2. How many teddy bears do you see?

I _____ four

_____

_____ .

3. How many blocks do you see?

I _____ three

_____

_____ .

Name ____________________

# My Trip

Write a postcard.

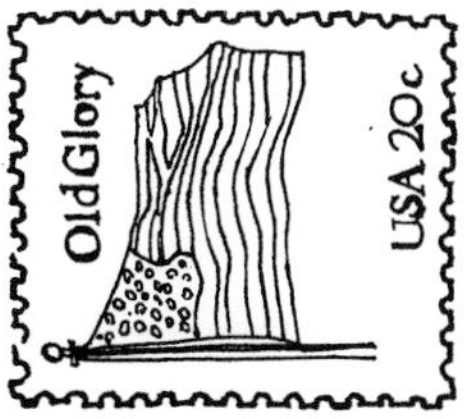
Old Glory
USA 20c

My Friend
300 Main Street
Happytown, U.S.A.
12345

Name _____

# Let's have fun in the sun!

*Fun* and *sun* have the same vowel sound.
Color each picture whose name has the vowel
sound you hear in *fun*.

© Scott, Foresman and Company

**98**

Name _____

# What do you know?

Write a word from the list to answer each question.

ears 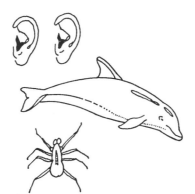    eyes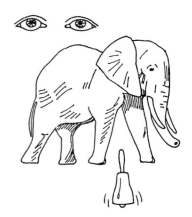

dolphin    elephant

spider    bell

1. What do people and animals
   see with?

   _____
   - - - - - - - - - - - - - - - - - - - -
   _____

2. What do people and animals
   hear with?

   _____
   - - - - - - - - - - - - - - - - - - - -
   _____

3. Which animal has very big
   ears?

   _____
   - - - - - - - - - - - - - - - - - - - -
   _____

4. Which animal can hear
   under water?

   _____
   - - - - - - - - - - - - - - - - - - - -
   _____

5. Which animal has eight legs
   and eight eyes?

   _____
   - - - - - - - - - - - - - - - - - - - -
   _____

6. What makes a ringing sound
   when you shake it?

   _____
   - - - - - - - - - - - - - - - - - - - -
   _____

Name _____

# Reading Objective: Recognize points of view or statements that are fact or non-fact.

Sample:

We all have five senses. Our senses help us know what is going on around us. Our eyes help us see what is happening. Ears help us hear sounds. The nose smells good or bad things for us. The important job of tasting is done by the tongue. Feeling is done by the hands.

In this passage the author thinks.

○  the nose smells only bad things.

○  the senses are important.

○  there is a lot going on in the world.

○  the ears do not help us.

If you chose *the senses are important* you are right. The passage does not say this statement. We can only guess this from the information given.

Name _____

# Try It

Read the story. Answer each question.

Most living things have five senses. People and animals have eyes. People need light to see at night. Some animals see very well in the dark. People and some animals have two eyes. Spiders have eight eyes.

Ears like eyes come in pairs. They work together to give us the best sound possible. Ears can also work alone. Each ear has all the parts to send sound messages to the brain. The ears of the frog and fish cannot be seen.

1. Which is a fact found in the story?
   ○ Ears come in pairs.
   ○ Frogs have big ears.
   ○ Eyes can be many colors.
   ○ All ears can be seen.

2. Eyes and ears are alike because
   ○ both are senses.
   ○ animals have them too.
   ○ both come in pairs.
   ○ they can feel.

3. Which one is a fact not found in the story?
   ○ Eyes come in colors.
   ○ Ears come in pairs.
   ○ Eyes come in pairs.
   ○ Frogs have ears.

# Months of the Year

Write the name of each missing month.

| January | May | September |
|---------|-----|-----------|
| February | June | October |
| March | July | November |
| April | August | December |

_____

January _____ March

_____

April _____ June

_____

July _____ September

_____

October _____ December

# Seasons

Finish each sentence. Use one of these phrases.

| in winter | in spring | in summer | in fall |
| --- | --- | --- | --- |

He can build a snowman

_____

------------------------------------

_____ .

She can plant a garden

_____

------------------------------------

_____ .

She can go swimming

_____

------------------------------------

_____ .

He can pick pumpkins

_____

------------------------------------

_____ .

# Dress for the Weather

Write the word that names each picture.

| cap   mittens   raincoat   shorts   sweater   T-shirt |

_____

- - - - - - - - - - - - - - - - - - - - -

_____

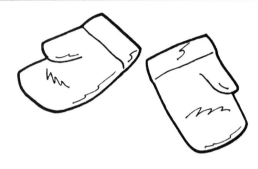

_____

- - - - - - - - - - - - - - - - - - - - -

_____

_____

- - - - - - - - - - - - - - - - - - - - -

_____

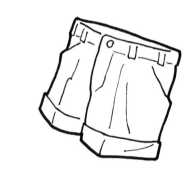

_____

- - - - - - - - - - - - - - - - - - - - -

_____

_____

- - - - - - - - - - - - - - - - - - - - -

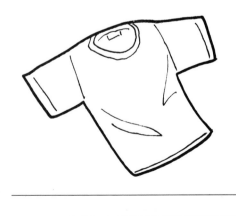

_____

- - - - - - - - - - - - - - - - - - - - -

# Whatever the Weather

Look at the words below.
Draw a line under the root word.
Then draw a picture of yourself in each kind of weather.

| | |
|---|---|
| rainy | stormy |
| windy | snowy |

Name _____

# How does a coat keep you warm?

Complete the chart.

|  | temperature of water with cloth | temperature of water without cloth |
|---|---|---|
| at start |  |  |
| after 5 minutes |  |  |
| after 10 minutes |  |  |
| after 15 minutes |  |  |
| after 20 minutes |  |  |

Write a sentence. Tell what you learned.

_____

_____

_____

_____

# Weather Symbols

Read the weather words. Look at their symbols.
Then write the word next to its symbol.

| | | | | | |
|---|---|---|---|---|---|
| snowy | | windy | | sunny | |
| rainy | | cold | | cloudy | |

Draw a weather symbol for hot.
Then label your symbol.

Name _____

# Today's Weather Report

Complete this weather report for today.
Choose a word to complete each sentence.

Here is the weather for this _____ day.

summer    fall    winter    spring

It is _____.

cloudy   snowy   sunny   rainy

It is _____.

warm    hot    cold    cool

The wind is blowing _____.

softly    hard

Draw a picture.

Show how you dress
for today's weather.

Name _____

# Who's dressed for the weather?

1. Fran dressed for a **winter** day.
   Use a blue crayon to color her clothes.

2. Dan dressed for a **spring** day.
   Use a green crayon to color his clothes.

3. Nan dressed for a **summer** day.
   Use a yellow crayon to color her clothes.

4. Stan dressed for a **fall** day.
   Use a red crayon to color his clothes.

Which child is dressed for the weather shown in the picture?
Circle that child.

Name _____

# Math Objectives: Demonstrate an understanding of measurement concepts. Understand possibilities and results of joining numbers.

Sample:

Look at the clock.
Then answer the question.
What time is shown on the clock?

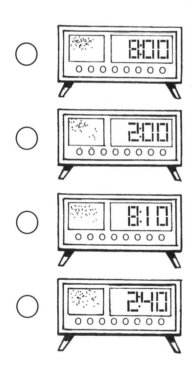

You got it! The right answer is 8:10.

Name _____

## Try It

Answer the questions.

1. What month comes between May and July?

   ○ April

   ○ June

   ○ August

   ○ March

2. What will the time be 1 hour later than the time shown on this clock?

   ○ 6:30

   ○ 5:30

   ○ 5:00

   ○ 6:00

3. How long is this pencil?

   ○ 5 inches

   ○ 2 inches

   ○ 3 inches

   ○ 4 inches

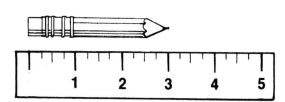

# Is it made of wood?

Some of these things are made of wood.

Circle each thing that is made of wood.

Then pick one thing made of wood.

Write a sentence about it.

_____

- - - - - - - - - - - - - - - - - - - - - - - - - - - - - - -

_____

# What can you make with paper?

Kendra *made* a *paper* doll.
Draw a line under the word in the
sentence that has the long *a*
sound you hear in *made* and *paper*.

1. Ned *made* a *paper* plane.

2. Ed *made* a *paper* game.

3. Jen *made* a *paper* cake.

4. Nell *made* a *paper* snake.

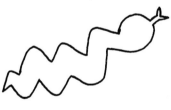

5. Fred *made* a *paper* whale.

6. Ben *made* a *paper* face.

# Save Trees

Complete the sentences.

| recycles | plants |
|----------|--------|

1. This family _____ a new tree.

2. This family _____ newspapers.

Draw a picture.

Show how you can save paper at home.

Name _____

# Ask or Tell?

Read the sentences.
Place the correct end mark in the box.
Use a ⟨?⟩ or a ⟨·⟩.

1. Why do people cut down trees ☐

2. People cut down trees to make paper ☐

3. The girls will recycle the paper ☐

4. How will they make new paper ☐

5. Can people protect trees from fire ☐

6. They can put out camp fires ☐

7. Can you save paper ☐

8. He can use the paper again ☐

# Alike or Different?

Look at the first leaf in each row.
Circle the leaf that is like the first leaf.

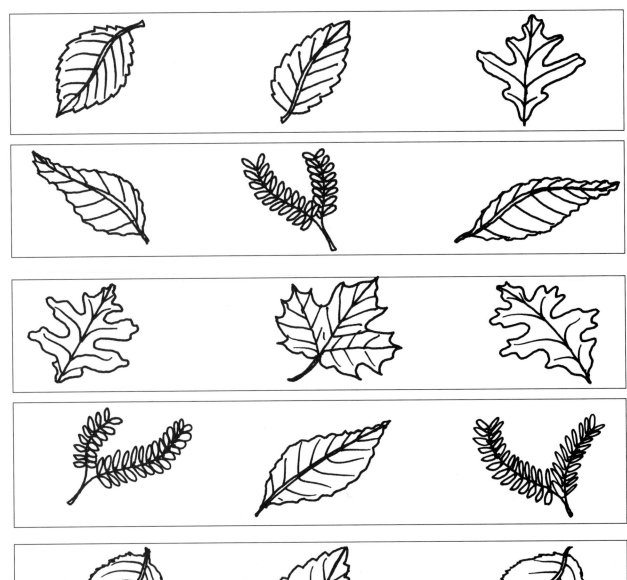

Write a sentence about leaves.

_____

- - - - - - - - - - - - - - - - - - - - - - - - - - - - - - -

_____

# Color Words

Choose a color for each picture.
Write the color word. Then color the picture.

| red | blue | green | yellow | orange | brown |

_____
- - - - - - - - - - - - - - -
_____ house

_____
- - - - - - - - - - - - - - -
_____ leaves

_____
- - - - - - - - - - - - - - -
_____ fruit

_____
- - - - - - - - - - - - - - -
_____ sun

_____
- - - - - - - - - - - - - - -
_____ moon

_____
- - - - - - - - - - - - - - -
_____ tree

_____
- - - - - - - - - - - - - - -
_____ cow

_____
- - - - - - - - - - - - - - -
_____ bird

Name _____

# The Biggest and the Smallest

Color the biggest tree green.

big

bigger

biggest

Color the smallest leaf red.

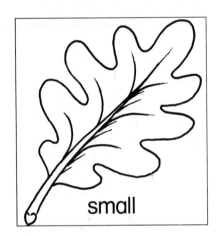
small

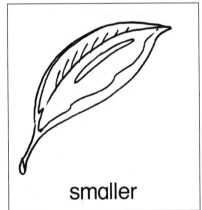
smaller

smallest

Draw three trees.
Draw a bird in the biggest tree.

big

bigger

biggest

Name _____

# What's that?

| blocks | leaves | paper | pencils | seeds | trees |

Use the words above.
Write the word that names each picture.

_____

_____

_____

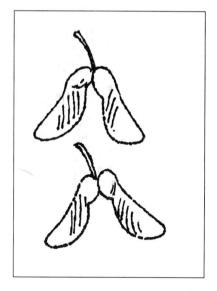

_____

_____

_____

Name _____

# Reading Objective: Summarize a variety of written texts and identify the main idea.

Read the paragraph.
Look for the main idea in the paragraph.
The main idea is the most important idea.

Sample:

> Trees help people in many ways. Trees provide shade on hot days. Some trees are cut down for wood. Other trees are cut down to make paper. It is important to protect trees.

The main idea in this passage is

○ Recycling is good.

○ Trees give us wood.

○ Wood can be cut.

○ Trees are useful to

people.

The best answer is *Trees are useful to people*. All of the other choices are important details.

© Scott, Foresman and Company

# Try It

Read the passage.
Then answer the questions.

## Trees

Trees are important to the environment. They provide shade for picnics or for sleepy cows. Birds use trees for their homes. They build nests on the tree's branches. Some birds build their nests high up in a tree.

Trees play an important part in the building of houses. Part or all of the house can be made from wood. Some people use trees for heating their homes. They burn logs in a fireplace.

In spring buds may appear on trees. People know then that warm summer weather will soon arrive.

1. The best summary for this passage is

○ People and animals use trees for many things.

○ Buds make leaves and flowers in spring.

○ Houses are made from wood.

○ Trees provide shade for people and animals.

2. What is the main idea of this passage?

○ Buds appear in spring.

○ Trees are useful.

○ Trees make shade.

○ Birds nest in trees.

# Word Log

These are words that I want to learn to use.

Name _____

# Word Log

These are words that I want to learn to use.

Name _____

# Word Log

These are words that I want to learn to use.